PURP

POWER

AND

POSSIBILITIES

How to be Happy and Successful

By Joseph Afolabi

CONTENTS

Part 1

Part 2

Part 3

Part 4

Dedication:

To him who is able to do exceedingly abundantly more

than I can think, pray or imagine

And

To the loving memory of my father – Abraham A Afolabi

Acknowledgements

This book is a synergistic product of many great minds, who share the same passion as me: the liberation of the human mind and spirit. They have challenged and encouraged me to begin to release my potential. One of the dimensions of my potential is this book. It is a proof and a testament that you too can achieve your dream.

I feel a great sense of indebtedness and gratitude to so many people that I have met on my journey in life. My heartfelt thanks go to everyone who helped me directly or indirectly, to inspire me, and contributed to the writing of this book.

Many thanks to the following for their indulgence and patient reading of the draft: Dr Carol Wolstenholme,

Marcus Wichmann, Rachel Hurt, Carolyn Bean, Darren Firth, Judy Short and my gorgeous wife, Sarah.

A big thank you to: my close circle of friends and family, my mum, Esther Afolabi for staying young at heart, Matthew and Deborah Afolabi, Joshua and Shade Gogo, the guys at 'Synergy' for their friendship, and all the members at NowChurch Langold, Mark and Carolyn Bean for their encouragement, Dr Glenn Balfour, Beth Mallender (author of 'A Fistful of Pearls'), Susan Barnett (author of 'Blue Settee') and to 'mum and dad', Pauline and George Hurt for their love and support.

I am very grateful to the people who gave me their time to answer my many questions, and also shared their personal stories with me. I salute your courage and determination for liberation, growth and excellence. Space and time would not permit me to mention your names individually, but you know who you are. Once again, I am grateful.

My gorgeous angel, Faith and my wonderful wife deserve another mention for their inspiration, love and support every day and in so many ways.

And finally to my source and the one who is always with me and the one who helps me to believe that NOTHING IS IMPOSSIBLE. Thanks for believing in me.

Foreword

I have known the author, Joseph, for the last seven years, both in a church context and in a professional graduate one. Throughout all of that time he has shown himself to be thoughtful, gracious, capable, and, perhaps above all, spiritual. With this publication he has brought all those qualities together – and more – to produce a highly motivational work. In this book, his desire to see others succeed and fulfil their potential is wonderfully expressed.

If you know the word over your life at present is 'potential', if you want to succeed in areas that up to now you have not succeeded in, if you want to be and do everything in life you are capable of, this book is for you! It is full of insights, wisdom and good advice. I warn you, once you start reading it you will not be able to put it down!

Dr Glenn Balfour --- Principal, Mattersey Hall

Preface

Have you ever wondered if all the billions of people on earth each have a unique purpose to fulfil in life? If it is true that everyone has a special assignment they were born to do, what is yours?

It seems to me that fulfilment in life and true happiness are hidden in the discovery and the accomplishment of one's unique purpose.

Why is it that some people seem to be without purpose and are constantly travelling through this life meandering along while others are taking each step of the journey majestically and with confidence?

How is it that the total of some people's possession are empty hopes and promises, and a broken heart that appears to be shattered beyond repair? Yet in this same world, there are those whose life is full of hope and happiness, and they often appear to have the courage to face life's challenges almost certain that they will emerge as winners.

We live in a world that is full of love yet hate abounds.

We live in a world that is full of hope but is also littered with despair.

While we're still pondering our failures and falls we are bombarded by the deafening sounds of joy and celebration of the triumph of a fellow human. And so the irony of life continues, but not without raising intelligent curiosities within some people who refuse to accept the status quo.

We all have within us the gentle but curious voice that tells us to refuse the status quo and search for our own path. It is as we take our own individual paths that we are led on a journey of self-discovery where we realise that we have the potential and the power to create unlimited possibilities.

I share with you on each page of this book, incredible truths, statements and universal principles that, when applied, have turned ordinary people into amazing achievers and champions in life. It is hoped that you will find strength and courage and be inspired to meditate on these powerful statements and apply the principles outlined in this book so that you may bring to life the amazing possibilities inherent in your mind.

After you have read this book, if you believe that you have a unique purpose and corresponding potential, and the power to be more and do more with your life, I shall feel that my sincere aim of writing it has been achieved.

I encourage you to dare to believe in the Purpose, Power, and Possibilities that are within you.

KNOW THYSELF

"…he who knows himself is enlightened;

he who conquers himself is mighty…"

---Chinese proverb

"If I died now I would be really mad!" Jane said to her friend, Neil who had given her a courtesy call that evening just to catch up and find out what kind of a day she'd had. They are both well over fifty years old, so they must have seen and experienced life to some extent, at least may be more than a twenty year old could claim.

As their phone conversation drew to a close, Neil asked why she would be mad if she died now. "I've never lived" she said. "My life has always been about other people: my husband, my children, my mum, my job and about lots of other people and things that I shouldn't even have paid any attention to. The truth is that I don't even know who I am and what my purpose in life is."

Isn't it sad and fundamentally wrong that people can go through life without really living because of the lack of understanding of who they really are? There are people who have become conditioned and constrained by life stories to which unfortunately, most have come to accept as their reality and the only option. The really sad thing is that this is the story of a large percentage of the world's population. In effect, this means that there are lots of potential creative designers, engineers, teachers, business men and women, authors, etc. out there who are stuck in the 'muck' doing other jobs that they absolutely hate and are paid just enough to cover their bills.

I guess sometimes it is easier to just accept life as it is served, but what if it is possible through the journey of self-discovery to change your life and fashion out a new path to an amazing and fulfilled one? I undoubtedly believe this is the plan of the Creator. What would you change about your life and lifestyle if you realised that you could achieve whatever you put your mind to? I have some good news for you – you have an incredible power, it's just that you don't know it yet. Within you lies the seed of greatness, just like the oak sleeps in the acorn and the eagle waits in the egg. The life you're living now is the one you have chosen to live, if you desire a different one, you can create it, the power is within you. It is true what Earl Nightingale said, "we are all self-made but only the successful will admit it".

We have all done it before where we look at other people who are successful and are excelling in their individual fields and we say "they are naturals!" almost suggesting that they were born with more abilities and knowledge than the rest of us. This could not be further from the truth. The poet and playwright, Maya Angelou, is noted to have said she dislikes it when people say she is a natural communicator. She often says "show me a natural heart surgeon". No one was born with knowledge or confidence!

We all have to first discover that we have the potential power needed to climb every mountain and soar like an eagle that knows its true capabilities. Unfortunately most people will remain blind to what they really could be and will never discover their true power and ability and therefore will end up in their graves with unreleased inventions, unsung songs and books that could have been bestsellers but were never written.

I feel sad and emotional every time I think about our lack of understanding of how much incredible power I believe the creator has deposited in human beings, everyone of us, regardless of culture, orientations or race. There's only one race anyway, that's the HUMAN RACE. We may have different 'colouring' and 'flavours' because of our varied experiences and personal stories yet we are all connected by ONE SPIRIT and essentially made with the same 'raw material'. What separates us is not a mystery; it is simply KNOWLEDGE - the power to be what you were created to be. The good book says "people are destroyed for the lack of knowledge". It sounds simple, doesn't it? That's because it is SIMPLE!

I didn't have any understanding of what it meant to study 'to acquire knowledge' when I started my secondary education. As far as I understood it, you just turned up in

19

lessons, wrote the tests and hopefully you'd pass. How wrong I was! When I saw my first report card and realised that I had failed most of the tests I started to think that I was 'dumb'. This led to me being put back from the third grade. It was the wakeup call that I needed, and with some help I started to put in the required hours of studying and practicing of sums. It wasn't long before I was hanging out with the bright boys of my school. It didn't matter that I was the youngest and smallest of them. My opinions and contributions started to count all because I had invested my time to acquire the necessary and relevant knowledge that I needed to excel in my exams. In some instances I didn't even understand the knowledge I had acquired but I had committed it to memory by rote learning. It felt like my IQ increased overnight, but what really happened was that I traded my time for something I wanted to develop.

I listened to one of Mike Murdock's audio recordings where he said "life is a constant trade act", if you want something, you have to trade your time for it. He went on to say "everything you don't have, you have been unwilling to trade your time for... time is the currency in the world of success".

What do you do with your time? Please don't say you don't have time. Everybody has an equal amount of time. The rich have twenty four hours a day just like the poor. The old have twenty four hours just like the young. Nobody has more time than anyone else. The difference is in what people do with their time. How much time do you spend watching television or doing other things that you can't account for? How much time do you spend with so-called friends who are not particularly contributing anything positive to your life? Do you regularly read or study to improve yourself?

It is estimated that one third of high school graduates never read another book for the rest of their lives. In 2009/10 almost 9 out of 10 (89 per cent) adults over 16 years living in England watched television in their spare time spending an average of three and half hours every day. Most people would rather buy multiple tickets for concerts or go to the cinema than buy a book that could show them how they can achieve more and be better at their chosen vocation. In just one year over 60 million people in the UK visited the cinema. It is a fact that people pay more for entertainment than they do for personal enlightenment and empowerment. This is not in any way a criticism of concerts or other forms of entertainment; it is just a statistical representation of current lifestyles.

If I gave you a chart to log your activities in a twenty four hour period what would it look like?

My 24 hours

Time	What I did
12 – 1am	
1am – 2am	
2am – 3am	
3am – 4am	
4am – 5am	
5am – 6am	
6am – 7am	
7am – 8am	
8am – 9am	
9am – 10am	
10am – 11am	
11am – 12noon	
12 – 1pm	
1pm – 2pm	
2pm – 3pm	
3pm – 4pm	
4pm – 5pm	
5pm – 6pm	
6pm – 7pm	
7pm – 8pm	
8pm – 9pm	
9pm – 10pm	
10pm -11pm	
11pm – 12 midnight	

You could try using this time log to see what you do with your time. Ask yourself if you're in control of your twenty four hours?

Mike Murdock, the author of *the law of recognition*, said "if you can't make twenty four hours go right, how can you make twenty four years go right?"

How many of the cells in the table will have 'reading', 'studying', 'learning', 'sleeping', 'watching TV', 'working', 'surfing the internet', etc?

If you really think about it you'll discover that most people want more money and happiness. They want to be debt free and have financial freedom so that they can do the things that they believe will really give them satisfaction in life. However, only a few people buy books on finance or buy tickets to seminars where they can learn how to generate more income or how to earn more working on a part-time basis. I can't understand what is so difficult about spending even just half an hour out of twenty four hours to learn something new.

Recently I had a chat with a young man who wanted to learn how to play a musical instrument. He told me that he was struggling to find time to learn and practice so I asked him if he'd thought about spending just an hour or even half an hour every day. I pointed out that if he practised half an hour a day it would amount to three and a half hours in a week. In a month he would have practiced for about fifteen hours, and double that if he practised for an hour every day. A lot can be achieved in fifteen hours. May be that is what you need too, just a short duration that is consistent to practice, sharpen your skills and improve, or maybe even learn a new skill altogether.

The Power of a Book

I agree with Aldous Huxley, the novelist and critic, when he said "Every man who can read has it in his power to magnify himself, to multiply the ways in which he exists, to make his life full, significant and interesting". In his book 'Think Big' Ben Carson tells of how he was an ordinary ghetto kid who transformed himself into one of the most celebrated paediatric neurosurgeons in the world, through the pursuit of knowledge and the power of belief. Ben and his brother like me and others I know failed at school for the most part of their education until a turning point came. Someone recognised Ben's potential and helped him cultivate it, he excelled and became a star pupil, and went on to become a surgeon. Ben was part of a group of pioneering surgeons who were the first to carry out an operation to separate Siamese twins where both children survived. Amazing!

I cannot state it in any clearer terms other than **knowledge and the application of it is the key that unlocks a completely new world of endless and amazing possibilities**: Possibilities such as where a man could be down and out one day and by the following week he is on top of the world, and is even able to raise other people up; Possibilities where a depressed and unhappy person discovers a deep joy of being alive and has hope for a better future.

I lived with all kinds of fear growing up. I had a fear of failing; I feared that I might end up alone; fear that my parents wouldn't be there when I needed them; fear of trying anything new. The list goes on. It didn't take me long to discover that this was not peculiar to me and that a vast majority of people live and breathe fear on a daily basis. Does that vast majority include you? What are you afraid of? Why are you afraid of what you fear? Is your fear and worry a product of your ignorance? Mine was.

My journey of discovery began twelve years ago when in a single year I read over sixty books and listened to countless audio recordings. I filled my mind with possibility thinking and then I started to believe that I could be who I was destined to be and achieve whatever I put my mind to. Everyone has a destiny whether they believe this and discover it, or not. Every person is unique and has a particular personality embellishment to them, which others can only imitate.

The truth is that no one can be you no matter how hard they try. No one can carry out your assignment in life the way that you have been designed to execute it because you have been wired with intrinsic details that no one else has. Just like no two snowflakes are exactly the same, every human being has different DNA and different finger prints as proof that there is something special about every individual. And yes, that includes you even if you find it difficult to believe. You are special and unique.

I understand that believing that you are special and designed with greatness within you can be the hardest and the most difficult thing to do, especially if all you've ever known is the exact opposite. I was born in a little hospital where my parents had to 'elope' with me because they could not prove that they had the means to take care of me once discharged from the hospital. My mother wrapped me in an old cloth then she looked left and right and once the corridor was clear she made a dash for the door and escaped from the hospital to walk all the way home having given birth to me just a few days earlier. My father was pensively waiting at home and hoping that my mum would not be seen escaping with me.

My siblings and I wore hand-me-down clothes and lived on leftovers from kind neighbours. I did wonder when I was growing up how and why we had ended up with nothing to our name and yet everyday lots of people drove past our one room home in nice cars that I had no doubt that they had worked hard for. I wondered how our kind neighbours always had enough food and could afford to spare us some.

My mindset was already becoming crystallised by the time I was four years of age. I saw, I heard, I dreamt of a life of poverty and low income jobs. It was a case of monkey see, monkey do. I was part of a life style and a culture that trapped and sucked its victims into believing that they had to die where they were born and that the 'the good life' was only for a select few, of which they have been unfortunate not to be part of.

I am glad that I have broken free from that mentality and I have met several people who have done the same. However, the pain in my heart still remains and intensifies when I think of lots of people who are still living a "zero life". A zero life means that there are no records to show that a person is here on the earth. Although they are physically here, they are not making the right marks and impact that they are designed to make.

That was my life at first. I didn't believe that I had anything to give or contribute to my community and the people around me. I was at the wrong place both in my thinking and in my actions.

What if you live your whole life only to discover that it was wrong?

Living a zero life is one of the tragic things that can happen to a person, why? Because it means the person has no record to show for their contributions because they were never in the right place of undertaking their assignment. They ended up at the wrong place, doing the wrong thing and perhaps, for the wrong people. Even though they did a great job, worked hard, maybe even to the best of their ability, but there is no trace of their 'timesheet'. It is just like being employed by an agency where you were asked to go and work in a toy factory but you ended up in a clothes factory. You walked into the factory, got changed into the work uniform, followed instructions very well, worked harder than anybody else, fostered an excellent working relationship with everyone, and then at the end of the working day you went back home. The toy factory where you were supposed to have worked rings the agency to say, "the worker never showed up and we are dissatisfied with your service". I can imagine the response of the agency; they will be very apologetic and say "well, since there is no record to indicate that our man worked for you that will be a zero amount to his credit".

What a waste! The 'worker' has spent his day and energy at the wrong factory doing the wrong job. What if this was you at the end of your life?

At this point in your life, you have the potential and the opportunity (like everyone else) to be who you were truly designed to be, but you're doing the wrong job, you're living the wrong life and heading for a future that you dread so badly (and you know it). So why won't you make a change? Oh you say "change is not easy". Change is not supposed to be easy. Can you really afford not to pay the price now? Would you rather choose to waste your potential and the greatness that you possess inside? What would it cost you to take the first step towards becoming the person you know deep down that you really and truly desire to be? Why will you not afford yourself the chance to unravel the real you?

Just to let you know, people are sick and tired of the fake you. Nobody wants the fake you who is timid and afraid to speak out; the fake you who has blended in and conformed. People want the real you who could introduce a different dimension and banish the status quo, and leave an enviable legacy.

Dr Eldon Taylor shared a story in his book 'Choices and Illusion' about an eagle who failed to realise its true potential. Taylor cleverly used the story to illustrate the

35

tragic end that often befalls people who go through life without recognising and accepting that there is greatness within them.

He described how the female eagle chick must have fallen from her nest at a very young age and ended up in a chicken yard where she was adopted by mother hen. The mother hen raised her as one of her own along with the other chickens, without showing any favouritism. The eagle enjoyed the warmth and the company of her siblings who were really nice to her. They showed her how to dig holes and wriggle down the holes to hide away from the scorching sun. She also learnt how to use her talons to scratch deep into the earth for worms, a skill for which she became a valued member of the family. She was satisfied with the security she got from her chicken siblings and adopted mother. They told her that "this was life and she would adjust in time". Nina, the eagle was impressed by the love and the generosity of the chicken family and accepted everything she was told as the gospel truth. Taylor added that the eagle's potential and her possibilities in life went altogether unknown until one day a male eagle flying overhead spotted her grubbing in the chicken yard.

If you are anything like me you are probably hoping for a happy ending at this point. An end playing out like this: the male eagle intercepted Nina, the female eagle, and said "do you not realise that you are a grand eagle. Why are you nesting with chickens?"

And Nina replies "thank you for telling me. I was beginning to wonder why I have these big wings and talons. This is my 'aha moment'. Will you take me with you?"

The male eagle then replies "it would be my pleasure to prove to you that you were created with unlimited potential and you are beautiful and capable to soar effortlessly to greater heights. Contrary to your thinking, you are not a chicken!" So they both flew away together and soared high in the mountain tops where they lived happily ever after. Unfortunately this was not the way Taylor's story ended. This is my alternative ending.

For some people my alternative ending is similar to their lives. They have had their thinking patterns interrupted, have seen the light and have made a conscious choice to accept and align themselves to their true and unlimited possibilities. It may have been difficult but it was not impossible. It may have cost them an arm or a leg but they stuck to it and transformed their lives. They probably said to themselves "I would rather die trying than die doing nothing, just like the beautiful butterfly must pass through the stage of the caterpillar before it can fly in its glory, I am willing to go through the pain and sacrifice the present to gain the future that I truly want".

Michael was one of my students when I taught in a state-funded school about twelve years ago. The vast majority of the students that the school attracted were generally lovely and with lots of energy requiring focus. There was never a dull moment in dealing with the students around the school. Although there were a few exceptions but they were neither clean-cut so you can imagine the day to day running of the school.

Having genuine interest in the all-round development and progress of my students and maintain a good rapport with them was something that was high on my priority list. I regularly capitalised on the opportunities Alison (my head of year) gave me to speak to students about what is possible and what they could be if they can only believe and work hard. I challenged them without holding back that they were not born to play a sequel to their parents' lives and that they could start a new chapter in their family history. Among others, I gave Michael one of the books that revolutionised my thinking and belief about myself and today I feel really proud of my students' individual achievements. Michael in particular has made the most of his life. He bought his own detached house at age twenty one. He is married to an amazing lady, Dani, and they are expecting their first child at the time of writing this book. His success story is a testament to the power of belief, and hard work and determination. He is like one of the eagles in life who realised that it was possible for him to transform his life. I cannot take the credit for the happiness that Michael has found and the successes that he has achieved. I don't even think that the book that I gave him as a present is the reason why he has done well for himself, but I do know that Michael changed his thinking drastically. He began to see his own potential and he believed more in himself.

Ian Berle, a friend of mine, was told as a secondary school youngster that he was tone deaf. He believed this for over fifty years of his life until that belief was interrupted by 'an eagle' who suggested to him that he ought to pursue his dream of being a saxophonist. Today Ian plays the saxophone for the band in his local church and at other gigs. It just shows that you can never create all your life's possibilities if you let other people dictate your limitation. Les Brown, a motivational speaker, often quotes one of his mentors who told him that "someone's opinion of you does not have to become your reality".

Some years ago a young man I know called Victor came to ask me for a job in the small business that I managed at that time. I told him that I could not give him a job because I believed he could do so much more with his life than be my employee. I almost heard myself say to him like Mufasa said to Simba in the Lion King "…you are more than that which you have become…you can do more with your life". Victor did go on to do more with his life by becoming an employer.

This is true of so many people who think all they can ever be is who they currently are. They have never challenged themselves with possibility thinking of what could be. May I ask you a question? When was the last time you set a time aside to THINK about where you are, where you could be and what you could be doing? Can you remember a time when you tasked your mind to provide you with the solution to a particular problem that has been hanging over you for a long time?

I once proposed to a senior lecturer in my high school that I would like to start a thinking club but the proposal was turned down for fear of the club becoming an occult group on the campus. I am certain that if people take the time to think about the possible solutions to a problem at a set time they'll soon begin to believe that it is possible to solve that problem and go on to have and be whatever they want.

The late Dr Albert Schweitzer, who in 1952 was awarded the Nobel Peace Prize for his philosophy of "Reverence for Life" responded to a journalist's question about what man's greatest problem is by saying "men simply don't think". Thinking and looking deeply within oneself not only creates enlightenment but also empowers the individual and opens up endless possibilities.

David J Schwartz in 'The Magic of Thinking Big' said "belief releases creativity". This was the case with Victor. I told him to do something I had read about in my favourite book. I told him to take a chair and sit outside at night and think about what he could do with what he had. I believed so much in the instruction that I gave him to the extent that I guaranteed that an idea would emerge in his heart and he will know that that is what he needed to give his time and energy to. Victor did exactly as I had instructed him to and sure enough, he had an idea to start his own school. The rest is history as they say. Victor realised his dream and today his school is still expanding. It's incredible what thinking about possibilities can achieve!

Joscham Dan who is credited with the strap line "at the root of every gain is the use of the brain" told the story in his book of how Bill Gates was known to have told his mother when she was calling for him around the house, "mama, I am thinking, don't you think?"

I wish every story ended like Michael's, Ian's and Victor's. Unfortunately they don't just as in Nina the eagle's case. In Taylor's version of the story, despite all the possibility stories that the male eagle shared with her to encourage her and enthuse her to look deep within and see that she was indeed a great beautiful and capable eagle, Nina still didn't believe it. She didn't waste any time in running back into the chicken house as soon as the male eagle stepped out of her way. And so it was that Nina, the eagle lived and died a chicken because that's all she believed herself to be.

This analogy is simple but appropriate. Put yourself in the position of the eagle and answer these questions honestly:

Would you have wished that you realised sooner that you were an eagle who is magnificent and can soar gracefully in the sky?

Would you have been happy if you had lived and died like a chicken when in fact you were created as an eagle?

I believe you would have been mad that you had lived and died without discovering the champion in you and how you could have used your greatness to benefit others.

Most people are never actively involved in the running of their own life. They let situations dictate to them the path they should follow. Whether it is in the choice of their career or family or even the day to day running of their life, they prefer to sleepwalk through life on autopilot being as passive as possible. Being on autopilot with life is like standing in the middle of a river with a strong current and refusing to make a decision which direction to swim to. The river will not hesitate to make the decision for you.

Some common human reactions to life include the reaction where people play the blame game and erect the walls of excuses higher and thicker than the biblical Jericho walls. They say things like 'I was born in a poor family', 'my parents did not look after me as well as they should have', 'I am not educated', 'the economy is bad', 'I don't know anybody who can help', 'I am single', 'I'm not old enough', 'I'm not good looking enough', and the list goes on and on.

Do you identify with any of these blames and excuses? Do you use any of the above excuses to place a limitation on what you can and can not achieve? Although some of those excuses may be true in your particular case, they are not potent enough to stop you from advancing in life and becoming your very best if you make a conscious and active choice. It's no use complaining and murmuring and blaming everything and everyone for your predicament. I guarantee you that there is someone somewhere who is making headway in similar circumstances to that which you face right now, but you have chosen to label it impossible. There is absolutely nothing that's impossible- impossible is something nobody has ever done until someone else gives their time and energy to it and then does it. The reason you think it is impossible is because you don't know who you really are and the incredible powers that lie within you.

PERCEPTION IS

EVERYTHING

I read James Allen's 1903 edition of 'As a man thinketh' and found myself pondering a statement he made about how a man only begins to be a man when he ceases to whine and revile, and begins to search for the divine justice which regulates his life. And as he adapts his mind to that regulating factor, he ceases to accuse others as the cause of his condition, and builds himself up in strong and noble cause. He no longer kicks against circumstances, but begins to use them as aids to his more rapid progress, and as a means of discovering the hidden powers and possibilities within himself.

Only people who have a deep understanding of themselves also understand that circumstances do not make the man. Circumstances only reveal the man's true power to him. David and Goliath's story is a classic example. David, the little shepherd boy knew that the circumstances of his having to fight Goliath the giant would prove that he had got the power to set a nation free. This story always makes me wonder what would have happened if many people, men and women alike, who answered the call of greatness had not responded positively. If they had not taken the time to discover themselves, to know and understand their assignment, the great purpose and the design of their lives, then the world as we know it today would not be the same. It says in the scriptures that "the whole world is waiting for our manifestations..." I guess the question now is: When are you going to emerge and manifest your inner beauty and gift?

You are probably thinking that there is nothing special about your life and that it is unlikely that you have a great purpose to fulfil. Do you know what? You are right! Because, you think it and believe it, you make it so. I know that sounds a bit harsh and depressing but sadly, it is true because as Earl Nightingale in 'The Strangest Secret' puts it, "we become what we think about". The great book says "... as a man thinks, so is he..." and James Allen expanded it this way: "as a man thinks so is he; and as he continues to think so he remains". Although you have greatness inside of you, unless you start to believe and think that way, the sad inevitable is imminent.

What will it take for you to change your thinking and begin to seek to understand yourself and the unlimited power that is within your reach? Will it be worth it if you become more than you are now and in effect do more and achieve more? Well then, this is your chance to do it while you still have breath and are still on this side of eternity. Get rid of your stinking thinking and wipe out the mind virus that has built what is supposedly a logical case for why you are not capable or good enough to be who you truly can be.

If you need to reboot your brain and reprogram your mind with new ideas and thoughts, that is what you must do. It is you and only you who holds the key to your incredible and genuine version. The Creator deposited that power within you. It is called the power of choice. What will you choose?

Let me reiterate that you have what it takes and you are neither too young nor too old. Zuckerberg got his breakthrough at age twenty and there are lots more who have done the same at a tender age. Colonel Sanders at age sixty five used money he had drawn from his first social security payment (pension) to pursue his passion of creating the now famous KFC chain of Fast Food Restaurants.

Excuses that people use are only as real and as strong as people allow them to be in their minds.

Knowing yourself is not being conscious and overwhelmed with a weak picture of you. It is not overrating others and short-selling yourself, and it is certainly not corrupting your mind and thoughts with everything that is going wrong in your life, and constantly telling everybody about it even to those who don't want to hear it.

Now you understand what knowing yourself is not, just do the opposite and find the things that you are good at. It may be only one thing. Magnify it and think highly of yourself not in an arrogant and proud way of "there is no one like me" but, in a healthy way of "I can't believe I have been blessed with this gift. I feel very grateful therefore I must use my skill well for the benefit of those around me". This is the first step to realising that no one is more special than you are. Our individual worlds are, as Earl Nightingale puts it, living expressions of how we are using and have used our minds. You create your world by using your mind well and making a demand of it to inform your choices of the things you must pursue. You will know, or at least have inkling about the thing(s) you are good at and must pursue by the passion you feel. Your passion and your enthusiasm are directly proportional to your commitment to be happy, fulfilled and successful in life. Les Brown puts it this way:

If you want a thing bad enough to go out and fight for it,

to work day and night for it,

to give up your time, your peace and your sleep for it...

if all that you dream and scheme is about it,

and life seems useless and worthless without it…

if you gladly sweat for it and fret for it and plan for it

and lose all your terror of the opposition for it…

if you simply go after that thing you want

with all of your capacity, strength and sagacity,

faith, hope and confidence and stern pertinacity…

if neither cold, poverty, famine, nor gout,

sickness nor pain, of body and brain,

can keep you away from the thing that you want…

if dogged and grim you beseech and beset it,

with the help of God, you will get it!

Once you've come to realise that there is greatness inside you, which is waiting for your permission to come out, and you consciously engage your mind and passionately employ everything that you've got, not allowing your focus to be broken, there can be no stopping

you.

What is the MIND?

Over the last century more discoveries about this empire called the mind have steadily been on the increase albeit only a small proportion of the world's population actually pays reasonable attention to learning the facts that have come to light about something so amazing which each one of us possess.

Recently I was privileged to present a talk to some men in a Connect Group on the topic 'What is the Mind?' It was an ample opportunity to share with the men, who were from all walks of life, what has become my passion – Learning about the power of the human mind and using the mind to its full potential in order to become the best that one can be. Robert Collier mentioned in his book 'Secret of the Ages' that "we as human beings are more than just beasts of burden who are doomed to spend our days in unremitting labour in return for food and house". If we could understand the power and the capacity of our mind, and appropriate it, we could take charge of our lives more and live like winners.

So how powerful is the mind?

Someone has referred to the mind as "the last unexplored universe", so let's find out some facts.

There are lots of fascinating facts available on the internet and in countless books about the incredible power of the human mind.

Here are some general and interesting facts that I found and shared at one of my presentations:

Did You Know?

The weight of an average human brain is about 1300-1400g – 3lbs i.e., almost one bag of sugar. It's smaller than an elephant's brain (6000g) but bigger than a monkey's brain (95g). A dog's brain weighs about 72g and a cat's brain weighs about 30g. Your skin weighs twice as much as your brain. The brain represents about 2% of your total body weight. It is roughly 140mm wide, 167mm long and 93mm high

Did You Know?

Neurons multiply at a rate 250,000 neurons per minute during early pregnancy. Your brain uses approximately 20% of the total oxygen pumping around your body and about 750ml of blood pumps through your brain every minute.

Did You Know?

Unconsciousness will occur after 8-10 seconds after loss of blood supply to the brain.

Information travels at different speeds within different types of neurons. Transmission can be as slow as 0.5 meters/sec or as fast as 120 meters/sec.

Travelling at 120 meters/sec is the same as going 268 miles/hour

Did You Know?

The human brain is approximately 75% water. The number of internal thought pathways that your brain is capable of producing is: one followed by 10.5 million kilometres of standard typewritten zero's.

(Source: Tony Buzan, Head Strong 2001)

Did You Know?

Your brain is capable of having more ideas than the number of atoms in the known universe.

(Source: Tony Buzan, Head Strong 2001)

More electrical impulses are generated in one day by a single human brain than by all the telephones in the world.

How much does a human brain think? 70,000 are the number of thoughts that it is estimated the human brain produces on an average day.

Albert Einstein's brain weighed 1,230 grams (2.71 lbs), significantly less than the human average of 1,300g to 1,400g (3 lbs)

If you could harness the power used by your brain, you could power a 25-watt light bulb

Did You Know?

100,000 = the number of miles of blood vessels in your brain.

1,000 to 10,000 = the number of synapses for each neuron in your brain.

100 billion = the number of neurons in your brain

When you were born, your brain weighed about 350-400g and you had almost all the brain cells you will ever have. In fact, your brain was closer to its full adult size than any other organ in your body.

And…that your brain stopped growing at age 18

Did You Know?

All of your "thinking" is done by electricity and chemicals

Mind over Matter ~ studies show that 50-70% of visits to the doctor for physical ailments are caused by psychological reasons.

Source: *www.thethinkingbusiness.com*

If you spend a little bit of time on each of these facts you will begin to see that you indeed carry inside of you a powerful tool that can create a world of wonderful possibilities for you.

I read that the "Mind," literally, denotes the seat of reflective consciousness, comprising the faculties of perception and understanding, and those of feeling, judging and determining. A linguist may be able to decipher from this definition what the rest of us may miss but that is ok as the main focus of our understanding should not be in the description but in the function.

I have over the years learnt that you can narrow down the functions of the mind to just two: memory and imagination. – Memory for your past and imagination for your future. And unless you have come to believe that your best days are behind you, I'm sure you will agree that your imagination is more important than your memory especially if your memories of the past are the things that are holding you back. This makes me want to ask you a direct question: WHAT IS HOLDING YOU BACK?

I believe strongly that the only enemy a person has is their MIND – the way they think. Les Brown often quotes the African proverb which says "if there is no enemy within, the enemy without can do us no harm". In essence, if your mind does not defeat you nobody else can. I am also reminded of what Eleanor Roosevelt said, "no one can make you feel inferior without your permission".

I was blessed in my early adult life to gain the understanding that if I think unhealthy thoughts about myself and sell myself short no one will raise the price. I don't know anybody who has ever walked into a super store and said "I think this box of chocolate is worth more than the price you put on it, can I pay double the price please?" It's just not done. If anything, you'll even prefer to wait for a deal - 'BOGOF' (Buy One Get One Free). Similarly in life, if you have concretised a negative belief in your mind about yourself, be rest assured that your life will ultimately follow in that direction.

An ancient truth which Psychologists and Philosophers are in agreement on is this: our individual life moves in the direction of our most dominant thought. So, why do a person's thoughts flow in a particular direction and how does a particular idea become dominant in a person's thoughts?

I always make it a foundational step for people I talk with to understand that no one was born with pre-packaged thoughts and ideas. So no one's mind works the way that it does because they were pre-programmed by the maker of mankind. The truth is, the way your mind works is determined by so many environmental factors – culture, upbringing, books we read or don't read, circle of influence, experiences, faith, etc.

You might be puzzled that I didn't mention nature and genetics, that is because I believe people use these as excuses for not striving to be their best and competing in life. They say "Mr X and Miss Y were born with their gifts and talents". Everybody is blessed with nature and genetics, having each survived out of so many millions of sperm, to be born where we were born, and to the parents we were born to. Once we have been born it is what goes into our minds that then set the stage for how our lives play out. – It is called the conditioning of the mind. Conditioning is a term I have borrowed from B F Skinner and Ivan Pavlov who both made it a prominent word in the field of human behaviour.

In one of my talk sessions I made reference to how anyone who has been to school would have learnt to read and write to some extent. Then I gave the participants a little exercise which was to look at a piece of paper, with something similar to the image below on, and tell me what they saw.

After looking at it for about two minutes they took it in turn to tell me what they were able to decode from the image. Their answers are probably similar to what you would say too. Do you see the arrow pointing down? Do you see something which looks like a switch? Do you see other weird shapes?

If these are all you can see, you are like most people who have been CONDITIONED to read images and inscriptions of black on white. Whilst all the images mentioned are present there is also the word 'fly' except that it is written in white, look again. Can you see it now? If not see the next page.

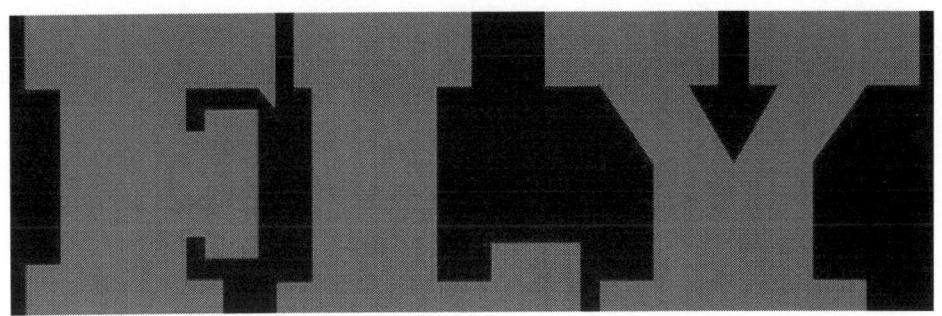

What about the diagram below, what do you see?

I am most certain that you can see the dot. Yippee! Can you also see the large space of white? I bet you can now. Well done if you focused on it before I pointed it out, it is very easy to only point out the little black dot in the middle of the box because it's the obvious.

You are on your way to challenging your conditioned mind. Just to show how easy it is to condition the mind I handed out a picture and immediately told them that it was that of an old lady. Like Anthony Robbins in his book 'unlimited power', I asked them, 'what kind of an old lady is she? Is she happy or sad? What do you suppose she's thinking about?

Here is the picture. Can you see the old lady?

These generated lots of discussions. I then handed out a set of pictures of another lady and asked them if they could describe the lady in this picture.

Look at the picture below – What do you see?

Nine times out of ten it is usually as I have expected it to

be. Most people end up only seeing an old lady in the

second picture as they did in the first because I have

conditioned them to see an old lady by the use of the first

picture that I gave them. Although this picture is actually

that of a pretty young girl, she is difficult to see once the mind has been conditioned.

Here is the picture again.

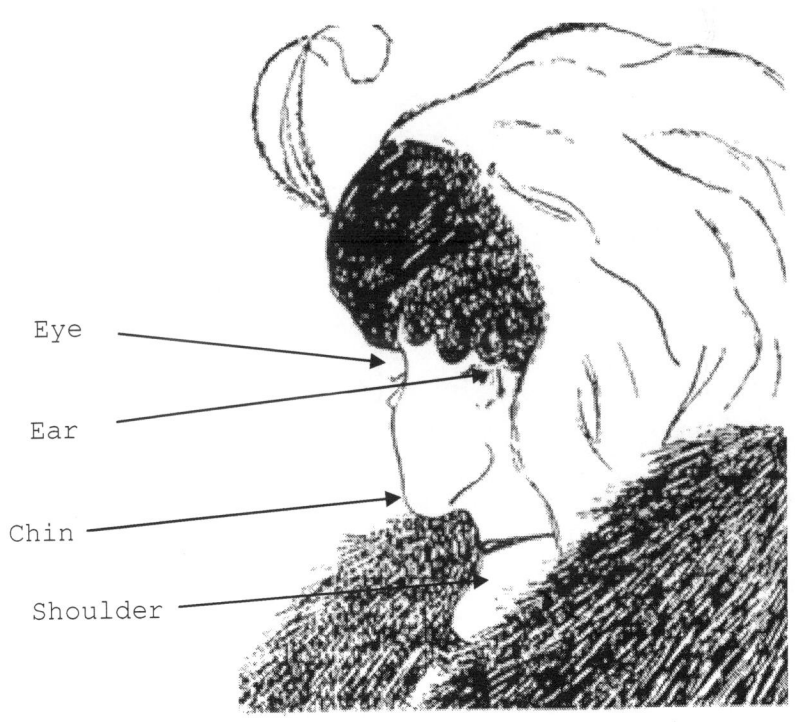

Conditioning of the mind solely accounts for what you see, how you interpret what you see, and how you react to what you see. If a giant harasses you, have you been conditioned to react by saying "he's too big, he's going to crush me?" Or have you been conditioned to say "he's so big I can't miss him if I hurl a stone straight at his forehead?"

What have you been conditioned to think about yourself? What have you been conditioned to accept about your past, present or future? What have you been conditioned to believe about this world that we live in? Do you think success and 'the good life' is only for a handful of so-called smart people? I say it again, NOBODY WAS BORN SMART!

The Mind is Malleable

I want to share with you four stories to show you how malleable your mind is and that if you change your thinking and the way you use your mind, you could transform your life into a happy, fulfilled and successful one.

One:

Ivan Pavlov was a Psychologist who was interested in studying the digestion of food in dogs, and during his research ended up stumbling upon one of the greatest discoveries of behavioural psychology which, he calls 'classical conditioning'. In Pavlov's research dogs were presented with food accompanied by bells ringing or light shining. The sight of the food caused the dogs to salivate. Pavlov then tried ringing a bell prior to giving the food. He noticed that the dogs begin to salivate just by hearing the sound of the bell. He extended the experiment by only ringing the bell and not presenting the food. Initially the dogs still salivated but it wasn't long before they learnt that the food wasn't coming then they stopped salivating and reaching for the food. So, even when the food was then presented, the dogs had been conditioned not to salivate and reach for it.

In your life what sounds, people, places or images do you have a conditioning with? Who, What, Where, Do you associate with good or bad, pain or pleasure, success or failure, happiness or sadness?

For me, it's the little hospital I was born in and the one room I shared with several others that I associate with abject poverty and obscurity. Unfortunately this is still the story of so many millions of children around the world. Children who have been conditioned to stop crying for help because no one came.

Two:

Zig Ziglar cited this second illustration in his book 'See You at the Top' and I have also heard lots of speakers use it in their presentation because it succinctly epitomises our lives as human beings. It is the story of 'fleas'. Naturally the fleas have the physical capability to use their catapult mechanism to jump about one hundred times their height. In an experiment, fleas were put in a jar with a lid on. For several minutes the fleas were jumping and hitting themselves against the jar lid then after a while they readjusted how high they jumped so that they no longer hit the lid of the jar. When the lid of the jar was finally taken off the fleas continued to jump just below the neck of the jar as they had become conditioned to jump significantly lower than their natural capability. The experiment also showed that when these particular fleas reproduced, their offspring followed their example of never jumping out of the jar.

What is the 'lid' that is restricting how high you go in your life? Who has placed a restriction on how much and how well you can achieve? Who told you that you can only go so far in your career? Why are you no better off than you were two years ago?

Have you not noticed that the 'lid' in your life is imaginary and that your limitation is self-imposed? Don't you think it's time to jump out of that jar and be set free to live to your full potential? I think it is time!

Three:

If you have ever been to a circus before you will know that they usually have an enormous elephant tied down by a piece of small chain that it could break without even trying too hard. So why won't the elephant break the chain? I first came across this story in Steve Berges book 'The Complete Guide to Buying and Selling Apartment Buildings'.

He told the story of how the elephant as a baby was held down with a tight small chain and wooden stake, and each time it tried to free itself the band from the chain cut into its skin around the ankle. The harder it pulled the deeper the cut, so the elephant's mind then became conditioned to give up trying to free itself as each time it did it produced pain from cuts in its ankles. The pain has now been engraved in the elephant's mind to a point that although it has now grown bigger and stronger and could free itself from being held, it will not even try.

When I shared this story with my focus group I was amazed to see how many people could identify and relate to the story. One of the huge pains in life is rejection from lots of people or from a person that you love and care about. Sometime it leaves an indelible painful mark to hear that you are 'useless' from someone you trust.

The feeling of failure especially when it's been more than once or twice can also squeeze out our strength and ability to succeed. You tell yourself "I just don't want to try anymore in case I fail again". "This is the reality of life" we tell ourselves, "there's only so much failure and rejection a man can handle". The truth is most people give up too easily and too soon. What we don't realise is that sometimes the last key on the ring is the one that opens the door. Most situations in life that promise a bright and worthwhile outcome, requires us to go the extra mile and be prepared not to take no for an answer. You know what they say, "the weight of a feather can break the hardest steel ever made". How does this happen? You keep piling things on the steel until it requires just the weight of a feather to make the break. For you that could mean: another trial, a different strategy, believing again, or taking one more chance. You never give up. You never give in. You keep going until you make it.

The same theme runs through these three stories that I have shared and that is: the injustice and atrocities we inflict on ourselves by allowing our minds to remain permanently conditioned by our environment, circumstances and the people we have relationships with. Let's be honest, you know that your life would be better if you could get rid of some relationships. You know that you would have done better in life if you had not met certain people, and you realise by now that the person you have become is as a result of the moulding and the conditioning process that you have passed through. We live out our lives line by line, scene by scene the exact way our minds instruct us to.

There are lots of things we can't control as human beings but there is one thing we can control and that is our mind. If we can take the time to understand its functions and the incredible powers we have we will live a happier and more fulfilled life.

Many people have struck a goldmine by their understanding of this truth. Others have transformed their lives literally by applying this wisdom. They have achieved happiness, financial freedom, marital bliss, climbed the corporate ladder and gone on to do what they really wanted to do in life as opposed to living a life of never happy and never having enough and merely existing. So many others that I know and have read about have been more than happy to share their wealth with others helping them towards their own liberation. This is what I believe in passionately and it is what this book is all about. My plea to you is to FREE YOUR MIND and EMERGE into YOUR GREATNESS!

Happiness and success has nothing to do with age. You could be sixty and be broke and empty or you could be eighteen and be a millionaire leading a children's charity that you have funded with your own money. It all depends on how well you use your mind.

To use your mind well to your advantage, and become a blessing to the people around you, there is a need to understand broad categorisation of the mind viz: the conscious mind and the subconscious mind.

The Conscious Mind

I have to hasten to add that the mind is not a physical thing like the brain. It is one of those things that you know you possess and it's there even though you can't point to it – it is somewhat spiritual. It is arguably the most important part of you. In fact if you do really want a transformation in your life here is how a biblical injunction reads:

...be transformed by the renewing of your mind...

In layman's terms, if you want to be TRANSFORMED, you need to RENEW YOUR MIND.

The conscious mind is our thinking and reasoning station. It gets its impulses and information primarily from our five senses. It is the part of you that tells you "that coffee is too hot. Give it a few minutes". When you see the date and realise you've turned thirty and haven't accomplish as much as you dreamed of when you were thirteen, the conscious mind is what tells you to give up trying and tells you that you are now past it and you need to opt for something different. If I ask you "what is right and wrong?" "Is it right for you to pay me for a job I haven't done?" Straight away your conscious mind goes to work to figure out an answer. The time you went to see a comedy show at the Apollo Theatre, it was your conscious mind that processed and understood the jokes. The conscious mind understands that you haven't been on holiday in the last four years because you can't afford it. In short it's the commander-in-charge of all your mental activities.

As you can see the conscious mind doesn't really do very much other than to respond to life's situations. And most times when it responds there is no guarantee that it will have lasting effect. That is part of the reason why for instance some people who know that smoking is bad for them can't really quit. Some even try for months and then they have a 'relapse'.

People hear shocking statistics like every pound you're overweight takes certain months off your life and yet they wouldn't change their diet and eating habit or even try and do some form of exercise. In fairness to some people, they set out at the beginning of the New Year to give up a habit and just about survive the first month of the year. Are you familiar with the term 'new year resolution'? Do you know someone who genuinely tries to ditch a habit or tries to change their life style but to no avail? May be you have tried to change your habit too. I can tell you this; it's never easy to break a habit without first creating the change in your subconscious mind and then filtering it through to your conscious mind (not the other way round). If you can imprint any action or change in your mind there is a very strong chance that you will be able to create the change in your day to day living. I've met many people who never give themselves a fair chance to succeed in 'resolution'. They failed before they even started because they constantly live in fear and they worry that they may not be able to achieve whatever they've set themselves. It is a terrible thing to live in fear of failure and constantly worry about every little thing. It takes the fun out of life and it can erase any chance of success that may be present initially.

Are you a worrier?

Here are some reliable estimates of the things people worry about; I first heard them in one of the late Jim Rohn's seminars.

Things that never happen: 40%

Things in the past: 30%

Needless health worries: 12%

Petty, miscellaneous worries: 10%

Real, legitimate worries: 8%

It means that 92% of people's worries are unnecessary.

Has it ever occurred to you that although most people know these estimates they still often live their lives in worry? I grew up in a community where usually the main worry was that of where the next meal was coming from.

Although most people in that community at the time had already been conditioned to only see so far and not have any particularly major aspiration in life, they didn't worry over silly and unnecessary things.

I have since learnt through my life journey and experiences to only concern myself with valid things. The thing I have the most control over is my thought so I choose to think on things along the lines of finding solutions rather than making mountains out of situations. This line of thinking puts me in charge and in control of life situations that come my way. And I tell you some of my previous life experiences and situations have been unpleasant and painful.

Wouldn't you like to be in control of your life situations? I bet you would.

The Subconscious Mind

I once heard a speaker said only two percent of the world knows that when your desires are different from your beliefs you will always manifest your beliefs.

I want to lay a foundation with the following story before we expound on the description and function of the subconscious mind.

Four:

This is a true life story about Nick Sitzman. It was published in the reader's digest some years ago and it has now been re-enacted and produced as a film.

Nick was a regular guy but also enviable for the right reasons, at least on face value. He was an incredibly strong and healthy railroad yardman. He had a great attribute of being friendly with everybody which earned him respect and admiration not only from his co-workers but also from his supervisors. More so, he was reliable on the job. You couldn't fault him even if you tried, well, so everyone who knew him thought. Unfortunately the saying, you can not judge a book by its cover rang true but only with negative connotations. Nick lived his life in constant worry therefore euphoric cadences always eluded him. As far as Nick was concerned, there was no reason to 'chill out', enjoy life and celebrate because 'the end' may come suddenly. In short, he was a compulsive pessimist who habitually feared the worst. One summer day, all the workers (Nick and his colleagues) were told they could go home one hour early in honour of the foreman's birthday. It happened that when the other workers left an hour earlier Nick found himself locked in a refrigerated box car which was faulty and had been disconnected. When Nick realised that he had been locked in, he started calling out for help and banging, perhaps somebody would hear and come to his rescue but it was never to be. It had been hours and by now his voice had gone mellow and had lost its power. His fists were bloody and he was completely overwhelmed with emotion and deep sorrow.

Nick believed that the temperature in the refrigerator was zero degrees. He thought "I am going to freeze to death if I can't get out." So he wrote a little message to his wife and family. "So cold, body's getting numb. If I could just go to sleep. These may be my last words."

The next morning the rest of the workers reported for work unaware of Nick's ordeal they slid open the refrigerator's heavy door only to discover Nick's body. He was pronounced dead at the scene. An autopsy carried out on Nick's body revealed that every physical sign showed that he had frozen to death but the strong disparity was that the refrigerator unit was not connected to the power therefore inoperative. In fact the temperature inside was about 61 degrees and there was plenty of fresh air. Nick's life had turned out in accordance to his deeply seated thoughts – A self-fulfilling prophecy arising from "what I fear the most..."

This true story has been used by business executives, ministers, educators, motivational speakers, life coaches, and others to illustrate the simple truth that your life is an exact representation of your subconscious mind.

I have also used it in this book because of how much it touched me. "What a loss!" I said to myself. I became genuinely sad because there are lots of 'Nicks' out there who are unaware that they are the ones creating their own successes and failures through what they permit to take root in their subconscious mind. No wonder the man who was known as the wisest man in his era, King Solomon, said "guide your heart (what goes on in your mind) above all else for it determines the course of your life". Whether you're happy or sad; whether you fail or succeed; whether you become rich or live in poverty: It all depends on what you harbour in your mind.

You cannot change your life until you change what you are thinking about daily. What you are thinking about daily is strengthening your belief system which has its station in your subconscious. Once it is established you are said to have developed faith (the evidence that something is real even though you can't see it). This is the point where everything begins to pull together so that your life actuality matches 'the picture' in your subconscious. The subconscious is not rational. It therefore will create and develop for you exactly what you feed it. This is why only about two per cent of the world's population write down their goals and read them aloud several times a day every day. It is no surprise that this percentage is the same group of people who are truly ruling and controlling the economy of the world and forging ahead in spite of the odds.

How to strengthen your belief

…faith comes by hearing and hearing…

What you keep hearing you eventually believe and what you believe will inevitably happen. You must have heard of scores of people who convinced themselves that they are unwell and in some cases even displayed signs and symptoms associated with a disease, although they are perfectly fine.

Are some of your predicaments your own creation? Are they something you've been saying to yourself over and over again? Are they just phantom pregnancies?

Some of the ways we say things to ourselves include reminding ourselves, through our thinking about what others have said about us. Why do you keep reminding yourself that your teacher said you can never achieve anything tangible in life? Why are you playing your dad's voice of disapproval in your head like a broken record? Why are you constantly thinking you don't rate? Stop it now! Give yourself a break and give yourself some credit for coming so far and start encouraging yourself that you can go the rest of the mile.

The subconscious mind accepts anything you put into it in the present and reproduces it in your future. The more you put a particular idea or thought in, the bigger and longer the effect reverberates in your future. It's as simple as the law of sowing and reaping. "...Whatsoever you sow you will reap". Garbage in, Garbage out.

All your actions and reactions are outflows of your subconscious mind. Although both the conscious and the subconscious are not mutually exclusive of each other the subconscious can often 'go it alone' leaving the conscious to play 'catch up'.

That's why sometimes you ask yourself, "Why did I do that?"; "was that really me?", or you say to yourself, "I didn't realise I could do that". Whenever you say statements like the ones above you are entering into the territory of the 'hidden self' as identified by Johari. The 'hidden-you' is that part of you that is not known by anybody, not even by yourself.

What is interesting however is that your subconscious stores every data imaginable about you. When you think you're in control and in charge of your choices, in fact what is actually happening is that your conscious mind is referencing 'the store house' to determine the action and or reaction to exhibit. Whatever choice you evince in that moment will impact on the design of your destination. Let me quickly say to you, don't panic! It's not determinism! Determinism holds that all events including human actions and choices have been set in stone and that nothing you do could ever change the end result. Although there is a clever Chinese saying that if you don't change the direction in which you're travelling you are most likely going to end up where you're going.

Psychologists at Yale University did some studies recently on how to alter people's judgement by 'priming' their subconscious. Afterwards, John A. Bargh, a professor of psychology at Yale, and a co-author with Lawrence Williams of the Coffee Study, which was presented at a recent psychology conference, commented by saying, "when it comes to our behaviour from moment to moment, the big question is, 'What to do next?' Well, we're finding that we have these unconscious behavioural guidance systems that are continually furnishing suggestions through the day about what to do next, and the brain is considering and often acting on those, all before conscious awareness." The studies proved that we have a subconscious brain that is far more active, purposeful and independent than previously known.

Source: http://www.nytimes.com/2007/07/31/health/
psychology/31subl.html?pagewanted=all

The Power of Purposeful Thinking

Did you know that you can improve your performance by thinking about it? Not focusing on the level you are at but totally focusing on the level you desire to be at. It is like the scripture says "… calling the things that are not as though they were…"

I don't mean thinking or talking about it just once or whenever it pops into your head. It has got to be deliberate, consistent, purposeful and wrapped with emotion (feeling).

Alan Richardson, an Australian Psychologist, carried out an experiment involving three groups of basketball players. The first group was instructed to practice shooting on the court for twenty minutes a day for twenty days. The second group were told to do anything they wanted except practising shooting the basketball or even thinking about it. The third group were told to practice basketball in their mind by just thinking about shooting the basketball for the same time as the first group.

The result showed that the group which practised on court made a 24% improvement.

The second group that was instructed not to practice without any surprise showed no improvement.

The third group which practised in their minds for 20 minutes daily showed a remarkable improvement of 23%.

Surprised? Don't be. The result again just shows the power of the mind. If you deal directly with the subconscious mind and engineer it with a line of thought, your whole being will move towards your chosen line of thought.

Guaranteed! Remember, "as a man thinks so is he and as he continues to think so he remains".

Where you are now is both physical and mental territory. The elements and the spirits of your current territory are happy to keep you where you are. That's why you may have heard people say they look back on about ten or twenty years of their lives and they can't see that they've made any significant progress. It is easy to fall into that trap – you just wake up in the morning; go to work; come back home (eventually); go to bed; do the same old things again and again. The only way to avoid this tragic trap is to consciously begin to think about a desired territory, and create mental or physical pictures about it, and talk about it for as long as it takes until you develop an invisible momentum, that propels you to take action to make it happen.

It's not a magic formula. It's just that the more you read, think (imagine), or talk about a particular thing the better chance it has to REGISTER in your subconscious mind, and once it has entered your subconscious mind, you will accomplish it.

Write down your Goal

Have you ever heard of the 1953 Yale study of goals? Although there is no proof that the study ever took place, what it claims to have found is fascinating. It is true, from that 'urban legend' and other studies that I have read, that no single individual or corporation wanting to make progress can diminish the importance of writing down goals and taking necessary steps towards achieving those goals.

A Psychology professor, Dr Gail Matthews, carried out a study that indicated that setting a goal, writing it down, and sharing it with others can empower us to achieve the goal. Of the original 267 participants, 149 of them completed the study. One of the groups from the 149 were instructed to write down their goals, rate their goals, write corresponding actions and commitment to their goals, share their commitment with a friend, and send weekly progress report to a friend. This group went on to accomplish 79 percent of their goals on average. I believe that an incredible unseen force is released in us when we start to read, think, picture and share our goals. We start to 'live' our dream on the inside before it then becomes manifested in the physical realm.

This is not new thinking; it has been around since time immemorial. If you can picture it in your mind's eye and you never stop thinking about it, talking about it and you don't allow your focus to be broken, your expected future will be created.

The Essenes Gospel of Peace is full of insights and principles about life. One of them is described by Greg Braden in his book 'The Isaiah Effect' like this: "an eloquent way of thinking that allows us to redefine what we experience on the outside by addressing what we become on the inside". The only way we can have our expectations and become what we want is by deliberately feeding our mind with the 'right stuff'.

Do you have a goal? Is it written down? Do you read it to yourself daily? Have you shared it with people you can be accountable to? Do you constantly think about your goal? If not, what do you constantly think about? If you notice, that is the direction in which your life is heading —"we become what we think about".

Below are two images. Which of the two would you prefer to keep looking at? How is each of the pictures making you feel right now?

Image A by: Andy Newson / FreeDigitalPhotos.net   Image B by: Maggie Smith / FreeDigitalPhotos.net

Unless something is seriously not right, you'll find that for whatever reason image B evokes negative energy from you and makes you feel a little bit weak albeit mentally. It follows therefore that what you continuously imprint on your mind can make or break you.

Mind imprint is not down to you alone, it's what others say about you as well. This is why it is of paramount importance to shield and guard your mind and only permit thoughts and pictures that will build you up and lift you out of where you are to where you want to be. Never let what people say or do not say about you be the main regulator of your happiness. Essentially your happiness should come from within, and whatever anybody else says should only be an embellishment of the real thing.

Play the Placebo Game on your Mind

Before you ask, let me mention quickly that the placebo has nothing to do with the placenta as one of my respondents thought. I carried out an unstructured survey to determine how many adults can claim to have a good knowledge of the placebo effect. I found out that one in five have never heard of the placebo effect. I am therefore going to take the liberty to talk a little bit about it.

I read in the Journal of the Royal Society of Medicine that the word placebo is the Latin for 'I shall please'. It was first used in the 14th Century to refer to hired mourners at funerals. It reminds me of the phrase 'the outsiders who weep more than the bereaved'. It is difficult to tell the difference between the real members of the family of the deceased and the professional mourners.

As a medical term, placebo was first documented in the late 18th century with Thomas Jefferson referring to it in his recording as 'the pious fraud'. Jefferson stated that the most successful physicians he has ever known assured him that they used bread pills, drops of coloured water, and powder of hickory ashes more than all medicines put together. Some hundreds of years later, most physicians still say they have used placebo in their practice because it works magic.

That's the end of my little history of the placebo. Now let's get onto the relevant and contemporary part.

I did not want to include the following information but then I realised that there may be people who won't mind being reminded about one of the most important findings in human science, and there may also be others who will only be coming across this for the first time.

Inside of our biological system lie natural hormones – chemicals released in the body as change agents. Some of the key ones said to be present in the brain identified by Dr Goldstein include enkephalin, endorphin, beta-endorphin, and dynorphin. All of these hormones serve as natural pain relievers that can be more effective than some of those ones advertised on our TVs. In fact Dennis Waitley pointed out in his book *Empires of the Mind* that later medical discoveries show that our bodies manufacture morphinelike hormones to block pain and give us a natural high.

A test by Dr Guillemin, who won a Nobel Prize in medicine for his work on hormones, shows that a single injection of endorphin he supplied gave cancer patients who had the injection a relief from their pains for up to three days, and fourteen expectant mothers also given endorphin during labour reported instantaneous and prolonged relief and went on to give birth to normal babies.

I know that it's hard to believe that we have inside of us such amazing medicines that can produce any physiological and psychological feeling we desire.

I read about a study in which actors were wired to electrodes and connected to blood catheters. They were then asked to perform various scenes. When they portrayed angry or depressed characters, their endorphin levels dropped, but when the scene required them to show emotions of joy, confidence, and love, their endorphin levels shot up dramatically. The study showed that focusing on positive thoughts can produce endorphins. Endorphins, in turn, can encourage feelings of optimism and well-being – this is the placebo game. In the placebo game you can be the director and the actor of your own play, and you can assign yourself a part that requires you to show positive emotions. The more you practice and rehearse 'your part' and 'your lines', the more it becomes a reality in your daily life.

Anthony Robbins in 'unlimited power' quoted Norman Cousins (Norman Cousins is known as the man who laughed his way to recovery) as saying medicinal drugs are not always necessary but that belief in recovery is always necessary. Although his story is unique it is not peculiar as there are scores of people who understand the power of laughter. It is no surprise then that the good book says a heart full of laughter is good medicine and works healing too. You know what they say, "you can not be bitter and be better".

I want you to take time to do further reading about the placebo effect to see how powerful it is and how you can use it to assail anything in your way of becoming the BEST VERSION OF YOURSELF. 'The Placebo Effect: An Interdisciplinary Exploration', a book edited by Anne Harrington, is a good one to start with.

If the placebo effect can be used to treat bleeding ulcers, alleviate pains from burns on the arm, relief pain from tooth extraction and treat cancer and other diseases then we have no excuse of languishing in unnecessary pain.

I am hoping that within these examples you're reading about that you will begin to see that you can take charge of your mind and demand of it what you really want in your world. The creator has given you all the raw materials, all that is left is for you to create a product and put your trademark on it.

I am about to conclude this chapter on the placebo effect but I can't resist adding the following studies as I find them very fascinating and cogent:

(1) Some patients who were given a placebo but were told they were given LSD had all the physiological effects noted with LSD.

(2) Ipecac syrup is used to induce vomiting and was very effective to the point where Paediatricians once recommended that it be kept in the home as a ready emetic for use in case of accidental poisoning. This is the same 'medicine' that was given to a 28 year old lady who was suffering from two straight days of nausea and vomiting. She was given 10cc of Ipecac and told it was a new drug that stopped vomiting. The result was incredible, in twenty minutes the vomiting had completely stopped and her stomach showed normal contractive activity.

(3) Dr Arthur Smith who himself is a survivor of cancer titled this next story as "what is wrong with Mr Wright?" It is the story of Mr Wright who was a cancer sufferer and was receiving treatment from the psychologist Dr Bruno Klopfer. Klopfer gave the account in 'Psychological Variables in Human Cancer' – A Journal of Prospective Technique 31 (1957). So let's see what was wrong with Mr Wright. Could it be the same thing that is wrong with the majority of the world's population?

Mr Wright had advanced cancer of the lymph nodes. He had received all the standard treatments possible and had become exhausted. He appeared to have little time left. His neck, armpits, chest, abdomen, and groin were filled with tumors the size of oranges, and his spleen and liver were so enlarged that two quarts of milky fluid had to be drained out of his chest every day.

News got to Mr Wright about an exciting new drug called Krebiozen, and he begged his doctor to let him try it. At first the doctor refused because the drug was being tried on people with a life expectancy of at least three months. Finally the doctor gave in and gave Mr Wright an injection of Krebiozen on a Friday, but in his heart of hearts he did not expect him to last the weekend.

Dr Klopfer was pleasantly surprised when on the following Monday he found Mr Wright out of bed and walking around. In the words of Klopfer the tumors had 'melted like snowballs on a hot stove' and were half their original size. Ten days after Wright's first treatment, he left the hospital and was, as far as his doctors could tell, cancer free. When he entered the hospital he had needed an oxygen mask to breathe, but when he left, he was well enough to fly his own plane at 12,000 feet with no discomfort.

Mr Wright remained well for about two months, but then articles began to appear asserting that Krebiozen actually had no effect on cancer of the lymph nodes. When Mr Wright, who was rigidly logical and scientific in his thinking, heard about this, he became very depressed and suffered a relapse, and was readmitted to the hospital. This time his doctor decided to try an experiment. He told Wright that Krebiozen was every bit as effective as it had seemed, but that some of the initial supplies of the drug had deteriorated during shipping. He explained, however, that he had a new highly concentrated version of the drug and could treat Wright with this. The doctor used only plain water and went through an elaborate procedure before injecting Mr Wright with the placebo.

Again the results were dramatic. Tumor masses melted, chest fluid vanished, and Wright was quickly back on his feet and feeling great. He remained symptom-free for another two months, but then the AMA announced that a nationwide study of Krebiozen had found the drug worthless for the treatment of cancer. This time Mr Wright's faith was completely shattered. The cancer re-grew and he died two days later.

What a tragic end for Mr Wright! If only he had the understanding that most of the time a medicine is only as powerful as you believe it to be; if only he realised that he possessed an incredible power to play a positive health and wellbeing game on himself; if only he knew that 'ordinary water' made him well the second time round and that it was his mind that turned the water into medicine.

All these examples and lots more that are case specific are available for our inspiration and encouragement to prove and ascertain an invaluable truth: The Mind is Powerful, and only YOU have the ability to use that power positively to your advantage or negatively to your destruction. Which one will it be?

Make it happen

Why are you so hung up in the 'now' and the 'present reality' when all the creator invites you to do is to embrace the future and the magic of possibilities?

You are holding this book in your hand today because 'I made it happen'. If I had never sat down to write the first word, which led on to the first sentence, which led on to the first paragraph and so on, it could not have been possible for you to be reading 'my book'. Writing this book has given me a fresh understanding of the power of consistent small steps. I now realise that you don't need to have it all figured out before you begin, in fact, nobody ever does. Every person who has achieved anything worthwhile always began with little consistent steps with the little resources that they had.

When you begin to take steps towards achieving your goals and you become actively committed to changing your life, it's only a matter of time before you succeed, especially if what you're thinking matches what you're doing and you keep your focus intact.

I have come this far and I still have a long way to go but it has been small step after small step along the way. I have learnt on my journey that I can not expect to win if I am not even willing to try. I've learnt, in the words of John Mason, author of *the enemy called average,* that 'I can not' achieves nothing but 'I will try' has wrought wonders. So, I made sure that no one can accuse me of not trying. Essentially that is what separates a winner from a loser. The loser waits for it to happen whereas the winner says; I would rather die trying and making mistakes than die doing nothing.

If you're always waiting for everything to fall into place before you start you will never make your dream happen. My favourite book says "if a man observes the wind and waits for all conditions to be favourable he will never sow".

I challenge you to dare to take the first step today. That could mean writing down your goal and answering one of the most difficult questions in life: WHAT DO YOU REALLY WANT?

Whatever that first step represents for you, today is the day that you must initiate a beginning. You do not have to know for definite how to get to the end before you begin.

Jack Canfield, co-author of *Chicken Soup for the Soul*, used one of the best illustrations I've ever heard to elevate the wisdom of taking small consistent steps towards achieving one's goal. He said imagine a car with its headlights on driving through a dark night going on a long distance journey. All that is required is for the headlights to be able to see the next one to two hundred feet. As the car makes the first one to two hundred feet, the light goes further to cover the next two hundred feet, and then the next two hundred, until the journey is complete. It reminds me of that old question, 'how do you eat an elephant?' To answer that question, may I refer you to an African proverb that you may have heard of. It says the best way to eat an elephant in your path is to cut it up into little pieces and have a bite at a time.

It is possible to make your dream happen. It does not matter how big your dream seems, what matters is for you to believe without a doubt that you've got what it takes to achieve it and start today with small steps using what you've got. When you look at your dreams and goals (I'm now assuming you've got a goal that you've written down), don't go into panic mode and become overwhelmed with your catalogue of excuses of how and why you can't succeed. Instead, what you must do is fill your mind with possibility thinking and say to yourself, ALL THINGS ARE POSSIBLE TO THOSE WHO BELIEVE.

Those who have gone on to make their dreams happen are no more special or intelligent than you are. It's just that you haven't committed the whole of yourself to only one thing. You've diversified and tried to put several irons in the fire. This is a common and costly error. It is costly because it is one of the major reasons why most people are never able to become their best in life therefore missing out on greatness.

Let us consider the following story which Robert Winston gave a great account of in his book *the Human Mind*. The story is about Herman and Pauline who were worried about their sixteen year old son because of how difficult he was. When he was born he appeared to have an overly large head with an unusual shape and despite the doctor's assurances, their son's head never shrunk to an entirely normal shape. "Fat! Much too fat!" was what his grandmother shouted when she first saw him. He went through his childhood years with a plump figure and was disinclined to participate in any physical activities or join in games with other children. He did not learn to speak until he was nearly three and he had a terrible temper which he displayed on one occasion by hitting his violin teacher with a chair. Needless to say she never went back.

He was the child that nobody liked at school and often talked to himself under his breath, always playing on his own (a real Billy no mates).

When he turned fifteen things got worse for him when his parents decided to move to Milan to pursue business opportunities leaving him behind in Munich to continue his education. He had lots of bottled emotions which he never shared with anyone not even with his parents. His letters to them were just to report that he was doing well in geometry. He eventually left the school after obtaining a note from the family's doctor. He arrived in Milan to his parents' dismay but there was nothing they could do about his arrival even when they found out that his reason was fabricated.

Whilst in Milan, reluctantly backed by his parents, he chose to write the entrance exam for a place in Zurich Polytechnic School. He did well in Mathematics and Science but didn't do so well in languages which meant that he needed to do another year of secondary education. So he enrolled for another year at a Swiss school.

In spite of all the 'natural oppositions', Hermann and Pauline's son finally gained entrance to the Zurich Polytechnic School and excelled. Today we know him as Albert Einstein who went on to become part of history as the most renowned scientist of the twentieth century and credited with the discovery of the Theory of General Relativity. He was dubbed a genius and ranks alongside Mozart, Newton and Leonardo da Vinci to mention a few.

When he died his brain was examined over and over again, but the findings were greeted with immense disappointed as they showed that there was nothing extra-ordinary or remarkable about his brain.

I added this story in order to discourage you from using 'intelligence excusites' as David Schwartz calls it in his book 'the magic of thinking big'. "I'm not clever enough". That is the greatest lie you can tell yourself. The world is full of lots of school drop-outs that have achieved massive success in all walks of life.

Just a few weeks ago I watched The Apprentice: You're Fired. Guess who was on the panel, Fred Turok, the chairman of LA Fitness. He was seen as the "thick one" in his family. One of his brothers is a Professor of Theoretical Physics at Cambridge; the other is an economics Professor now working with the South African government. But Fred who suffered from undiagnosed dyslexia was finally permanently expelled from school after working his way through 11 different schools. Today Fred has made his dream happen in spite of his inability to settle at school as a youngster.

I read the story of someone who suffered from learning disabilities and difficult motor coordination as a child. He did not learn to tie his shoe laces until he was about nine and was labeled mentally retarded by his elementary school teachers. When he was eventually diagnosed with dyslexia he sought necessary help, learnt and did what he needed to do to succeed academically. He finished college with good grades and proceeded further to study law. He passed his bar exam and became a prosecutor. Dan Malloy has made his dream happen. He was sworn in as the Governor of Connecticut in January 2011.

There is really no excuse for not making your dream happen. J K Rowling, author of Harry Potter series made her dream happen whilst receiving state benefits. The late

Mary K Ash, founder of Mary K Cosmetics; Richard Branson, the business magnate; Alan Sugar, also a business magnate; Myles Munroe, the minister from the Bahamas; and Les Brown, a bestselling author (who was also labeled educable mentally retarded but today has become one of the top five motivational speakers in the world), and many more, all these people have one thing in common – THEY MADE IT HAPPEN despite lack of conventional education and privileges. They did not inherit any pot of money from their parents. Nobody will achieve your goals for you and make your dreams happen. You are the only one who has that responsibility so, accept the call, focus on the end result and take the first step today no matter how small it seems.

I listened to Paul Scanlon, a minister in a teaching inspired by Susan Jeffers' book 'Feel the Fear and Do it Anyway', and I immediately ordered the book. The book which has become a classic, and recently celebrated twenty five years of publication, is still helping many people to face their fears and still march on taking small steps to making their dreams happen. Susan Jeffers herself was turned away by many publishers and almost gave up on her dream of becoming an author. One of the rejection letters she received said that if a particular famous princess who is now deceased were cycling nude down the street giving the book away nobody would read it. How wrong! The book has sold millions of copies and has changed millions of lives.

I'm reminded also of Dr Seuss in his attempt to become an author. Although the book he was trying to get published, *Mulberry Street* is a delightful peek into the vivid imagination of a child, publishers in 1937 were not so receptive; in fact, Dr Zeus presented his manuscript to 27 publishing houses and received 27 rejections. Although discouraged, he never gave up. His books have now been translated into fifteen different languages and have sold over two hundred million copies from about sixty published books.

It seems to me that successful people were failures who stuck at it until they metamorphosised into enviable achievers.

I am sure you've heard of Beethoven. As a child he handled the violin awkwardly and preferred playing his own compositions instead of improving his techniques. His teacher called him a hopeless composer. Beethoven made his dream happen by writing some of the greatest symphonies despite being completely deaf.

How would you like to pay approximately fifty pounds for an original painting by Van Gogh? 'Yes please', I hear you say. That was the price a sister of one of Van Gogh's friends paid for his painting and she only did it out of pity for him. This didn't stop Van Gogh from completing over eight hundred paintings. One of his paintings alone, 'the starry night' is now worth one hundred and forty million dollars.

Greatness is always guaranteed to tenacious individuals, like the English novelist John Creasey who got 743 rejection slips from publishers before still going ahead to publish about 600 books, and selling over 80 million copies.

In order to make it happen, you have to keep at it, setting your face like a flint and only having eyes on the goal telling yourself FAILURE IS NOT AN OPTION. Sticking at it and never giving up is the name of the game. When you try and fail (and it doesn't matter how many times you tried), you must never see yourself as a failure, only see an attempt that went wrong. Try and learn something new in every attempt and just keep going until you make it happen.

Lesson from the Chinese Bamboo Tree

What lesson can we learn from the way Chinese bamboo trees grow? Well, as it turns out, there is a lot to learn. Pay attention to it as this may hold the key to you changing your life and making your dream happen.

The Chinese bamboo tree is an unusual plant in the sense that when planted it doesn't break through the ground for the first four years. It starts to grow properly in the fifth year having been watered and fertilised consistently for the last five years, it grows 90 feet in six weeks of the fifth year. Incredible! It looked like nothing was happening in the first four years. At that point it's not uncommon to begin to think that it might be a better idea to try something else – but that is why most people fail in life -lack of focus and persistence. Calvin Coolidge said "nothing in the world can take the place of persistence. Talent will not; nothing is more common than unsuccessful men with talent..." Don't be one of the people who have talent and greatness inside of them but still end up unsuccessful and a failure in life because they gave up too soon.

As a youngman of eighteen, I found myself listening to Don Williams and I recall one of his songs where he sang "pressure makes diamond much harder than stone..." and that has stuck with me all these years challenging me to never give up in the face of hardship. Also Reading Robert Schuler's 'Tough Times Never Last, but Tough People Do!' has kept me fired up whenever I think of retiring and resigning to 'fate'. It's easy to give up trying and be 'content', especially in my case: I have a good job that pays well; I have a beautiful wife; My gorgeous 'angel', Faith who is three years old makes me laugh and oozes out lots of positive energy on a daily basis; so I could easily give up trying anything else and settle for what I have. But I dislike 'fate' with a passion. I think it's a man's lazy way of throwing away his destiny into a deep sea and expecting the destiny to swim back out craving for a warm embrace. If you want to make it happen for you, you have to keep on fighting for it and program yourself to believe that inside of every hardship and problem lies a massive opportunity. You just have to look hard enough in order to see it.

Think yourself out of the recession

Most people will see times of recession as the time when everything comes to a grinding halt but some other people will view it differently and seek out the hidden opportunities and the new openings. The late Jim Rohn was known for saying "recession restores resourcefulness" and indeed it is so. I know someone called David Barker who decided to train as a teacher after his family's small business was hit hard by recession. Today David has achieved his dream of becoming a teacher and he also became the first university graduate of his family.

I heard the story of a couple who were badly affected by the recession but started selling handmade bracelets which they make in their living room. In the first few months of starting their business, they made a profit of about one to two thousand – Not bad for a product they make in their living room!

Did you know that some of the world's big companies started during a recession period? General Electric Co. was established in 1876 in the middle of the panic of 1873, a six-year recession. Thomas Edison did not give in to the prevalent hardship and panic of the era but went on to establish a company which today employs people from around the world. Other companies that started during a time of global financial hardship include Burger King, Hewlett Packard (which apparently had a mere investment of $538), Microsoft Corporation, CNN, and lots more. You just have to type 'companies that started in a recession' into a search engine and you'll see dozens. Recession forces people to have time-out and causes them to take an inventory of their skills and compels them to become more creative.

So, are you going to give up on your dream just because recession is plastered all over the news? Let's even say you've lost your job, do you know that you can buy a pallet of goods for approximately £200 and by the time you sell the items on the pallet individually on Ebay or Amazon you could be in profit two or three times your initial investment?

There are hundreds of ideas on how to make money without leaving your home. There was a time I learnt to make a thousand pound a day or at least two hundred pounds a day. I still have those skills but I don't use them now for internal personal resolve – (money is a good servant but a bad master!).

Anyone can achieve whatever they put their mind to. You may fail once, twice or even three times but it doesn't mean that you won't succeed if you carry on trying. Thomas Edison said the reason men fail is broken focus. We have to choose to keep trying and never give up. There is a reason why the maker gave us the power of choice and he urges us to choose life and peace.

You are who you learn to be. You can either learn to be someone who gives up because 'it's hard' or you can learn and choose to toughen up and say to yourself "I am not going to give up, I will make my dream happen!"

I watched an interview with Michael Jordan where he said "you miss every shot you don't take". I believe this applies directly to life. How many missed opportunities do you now wish you had acted upon? Have you missed any shots in life? Are there things you wished you had done?

Everyone at one time or another has missed a shot or two in life so it's not peculiar to you alone. The good news now is that you are learning from this book that no one can make your dream happen for you. You have to pluck up courage, be bold and take another shot at your dream. If for any reason or excuse you say pass on your 'shot' and 'dream' then, the dream will die with you. Imagine if Henry Ford as a broke mechanic in his forties never took a step towards making his dream happen. We probably wouldn't be enjoying his creation as we do today. We can get into a car and be at our destination in less time than it would take riding on a camel.

Are you prepared to take as many shots as it takes until you make your dream happen? Well, the ball is in your court. MAKE IT HAPPEN TODAY.

Making your dream happen does not have to be a daunting ordeal. In many cases, people who have made their dreams happen have not had to start from the bare minimum or completely reinvent themselves. They have simply been flexible and adaptable and have only transferred the skills and energy they already possess into something else they truly desired to do. It could be that someone who enjoys getting friends together for a meal realises that they can become an event organiser; A nursery school teacher who loves making up his own story in his lessons decides to become an author of children's books; or to be like Mr Les Brown who turned his Disc Jockey skills into public speaking and has now spoken to millions of people inspiring them and challenging them appropriately. Do you have skills that you know could be better used somewhere else? Why aren't you using them? Are you worried that you don't have the expertise? Well learn then. Sometimes you don't even need the expertise to make a start. You can start and then learn on the job. All you have to do is just believe in yourself enough to take the first step.

I learnt in my leadership classes that the best thing you can do for yourself is to take an honest inventory of your life and identify your assets as well as your weaknesses. It is called a SWOT analysis. I can see the advantages of doing a SWOT but if care is not taken your mind will naturally dwell on your weaknesses especially if someone like your parents, teachers, bosses or even friends have pointed it out to you before. My take on looking at your Strengths, Weaknesses, Opportunities and Threats is to focus intensely on your strengths and that will compensate for your weakness and the things you're not good at. As you may be aware, the Chinese table tennis national team has won 38 world championships and 15 Olympic gold medals even though the players are not good at using their backhands. A reporter caught up with one of the coaches and asked how they have managed to stay as world champions with the players not being good at using their backhand. The coach replied, "We concentrate on the players' forehand and sharpen it so it compensates for the backhand". It works all the time, pay attention to what you're good at. Improve on it everyday. Stay in the centre of your expertise and you'll stay out of your weakness. It's like light and darkness. Darkness is just the absence of light. The more light you have the less darkness you experience. If you can concentrate on what you've got going for you and you can continue to sharpen and increase it, there is no limitation to where you can go or what you can do.

Cliff Young, the Australian credited with 'the young shuffle', a style of running long distance races, is an average farmer. He is a man who really understood what it means to believe in yourself and use what you've got to make a dream happen.

In 1983 Cliff turned up for the annual ultra-marathon which involves running 543.7 miles from Sydney to Melbourne. He was wearing overalls and his work boots and later confirmed his age as 61. Everyone was shocked when they realised that Cliff wasn't there to be a spectator but rather to participate. "You can't be serious." They said to him. "This is a race that takes five days to complete and only world-class athletes who train especially for it ever take part." Cliff was not to be intimidated by all those facts including, seeing that typically all the athletes were less than thirty years old and had big companies as their sponsors. He ignored all that he could see and just focused on taking part in the race. When he was asked what his strategy for completing the race was going to be he simply replied, "...I grew up on a farm where we couldn't afford horses or tractors, and the whole time I was growing up, whenever the storms would roll in, I'd have to go out and run up the sheep. We had 2,000 sheep on 2,000 acres. Sometimes I would have to run those sheep for two or three days. It took a long time, but I'd always catch them. I believe I can run this race." As you can imagine, no sooner than the race started than all the pros dashed off and Cliff was left behind just shuffling along. Cliff went on to win the race because he 'shuffled' throughout the race, never stopping for any rest at all. He was the first one to cross the finish line and created a new world record in the process. Cliff had transferred his skill and energy for rounding up sheep on the farm to the platform of an ultra-marathon and won in an outstanding way.

154

You too can start using what you already have to begin to build a future that you desire. Remember that the future is not somewhere we're going. The future is somewhere we create. You have got what it takes to make your dream happen. You just have to take the first step TODAY! If you don't start, you can never finish. That means five years down the line, you will still be where you are now. The very first step of cause is to have a goal and write it down. At this point I strongly suggest that you put this book down, get a pen and a piece of paper and write down your goal if you haven't already done it. The good book says, write the vision down so that he who reads it can take it seriously and make haste in accomplishing it. Once you've written it down, you need to read it to yourself at least once every day. I have already mentioned about the power of sharing your goal with people you can be accountable to. As you read it out loud to yourself more and more and you talk about it with people, the way and how to accomplish it will present itself to you. It happens all the time. It's a natural law of collocation and sequence. What you do first determines what happens next. Reading your goal out aloud is like sowing a seed and the more you read it the deeper it takes root.

You Can Buy Happiness And Secure Your Future

...perhaps the true measure of how rich you are is shown by how many people you reach

Long before I made my dream happen with the help of those in my inner circle, my life was characterised by lots of days without eating any meal, not because I was abstaining from food but because I couldn't afford to feed myself. I recall one of the occasion to be when I was in a tertiary college studying for a certificate in Education. I had gone two days without any food whatsoever and I was on my third day when I got an invite to go for a meal with some other students to one of my lecturer's house. When we got to his house his wife had already prepared the meal so we only had to sit down and enjoy it. I was the only one whose plate looked so clean by the end you would think it had been through the dishwasher. It's now been twenty three years since that kind gesture was shown to me by my then lecturer and his family and I still remember it in detail now, and my heart is still full of gratitude to them.

I have since had lots and lots of other help from other people I have met on my journey through this life, but the most fulfilling thing for me is that I have also learnt that the reason I have what I have is so I can SHARE it with others who don't have anything at all or who perhaps just need a little more to help them get to where they need to be. For me now, the highest form of success is helping other people succeed. I believe that we were all made to help each other.

If you look back on your life there's no doubt you'll be able to make a list of people who have helped you along the way. Even if you are one of those who usually say "no one has ever given me anything in my life", you will still realise that if you take a sincere look at your life's journey there was always someone there helping you along the way.

For some it could be your parents, your teacher, your friend, or your spouse. In my case, my uncle, David, is one of those who helped and inspired me. Being a late starter in life himself, he went on to qualify as a chartered accountant and worked for major accounting firms, including KPMG, in senior positions. Today he is travelling around the world on business trips and multiplying his success doing what he does best which is, helping others to achieve success. As a landlord, he tells tenants who are struggling to feed their family not to worry about house rent but just to concentrate on feeding their children and pay rent when conditions become favourable. I have lost count of how many people he has sponsored through school, some to university level. For him, life is like riding a horse, if the horse throws you off; you get back on it by yourself or get someone to help you get back on it. He believes that the person who helps another is privileged and they should count it a great honour to serve humanity. It reminds me of what Horace Mann said, "We should be ashamed to die until we have won some victory for humanity..."

Have you won any victory for the people around you and given someone a much desired help? It's not too late if you haven't and if you have, well done. Keep it up. That is the only thing that guarantees the best feeling.

A study was done recently on how money can indeed buy happiness. I know we all grew up hearing that money won't make you happy but Mike Murdock was quick to say poverty won't make you happy either. The result of the study which Michael Norton presented was full of fascinating statistics most of which only a few people already know and practice in their day to day living. The main implication of the result is that if all you think about is "I, me and myself" then you can not avoid misery. You will be like the Dead Sea, always receiving but having no outlet stream. Can you imagine filling up on all those gorgeous meals and not letting anything out by way of excretion?

Norton said they found that the participants in their study who were given money to spend on charitable donations and buying gifts or meals for others displayed a higher level of happiness and satisfaction in comparison to the other participants who spent their money on themselves, even when they had used the money on something they genuinely needed.

As an eligible (ish) bachelor living alone in my flat in Tooting, London, I used to be so emotional whenever I sat down to eat the food that I had prepared all by myself. Did I mention that I can cook? I could give Jamie Oliver a run for his money but we'll have to leave that for another time. After I sat down to eat, I often got overwhelmed by the fact that I knew that somebody was out there who had no food and didn't have any help at hand. I would become upset and eat the food with a heavy heart and equally be full of gratitude for being so privileged.

In 2005 I had the most amazing opportunity to put my money where my mouth is. I took my whole salary and headed for a West African country that had just been hit by one of the worst famines, to help the people of a village in my own little way. With the help of some friends, like Mel and Darren who donated £300, I was able to provide bags of food to all the people in the village and also help out in an orphanage and a local school, where the only motivation for children to attend school was because they would be fed. It turned out to be one of the BEST things I have ever done in my entire life for which I am very grateful. I have now resolved without an iota of doubt that true happiness comes from helping others. And there's no better time to help others than when you need help yourself. Helping others at a time when you need help yourself can be difficult but it's always worth it in the end.

There is a special kind of elated joy that follows seeing somebody happy because of something you've given them. Lives have been saved by the kindness of strangers. People have had life transforming experiences and opportunities given to them by other people who care.

Why do you think some employees pledge allegiance to their companies and work as hard as they possibly can? It's because their company showed an interest in their all-round progress, invested in them and empowered them so that they could become the best they can be. I believe that one of the ways an employer can get the best out of an employee is to train and invest in them, not just to pay them a higher salary. Similarly, there is something magical about the two-sided coin of helping somebody to make their dream come true. On the one side of the coin, you experience true happiness, while on the other side of the coin the person you helped will enrich your life directly or indirectly.

It's time to begin to seek out people who need your help to survive and make it to the next phase of their life. You may not be able to help everybody or you may even feel inundated by the long list of people you think need your help. The best you can do is to start with the first person and give them all the help you can give them. Do it while you've still got the opportunity because in reality when you're dead and gone, the only people that will fondly remember you are the people who benefited from you and depended on your goodwill.

It is crucial for you to understand that one of your missions in life is to raise somebody up. There is a beautiful rendition of 'you raise me up' by Josh Groban. It makes me well up every time I listen to it. It also makes me grateful that somebody helped me get to where I've got to today. At the same time I think of people who wouldn't make it out of the shackles of ignorance and darkness; people who were born into poverty and seem to be destined to die in it; people who won't have the chance to shine in life because you and I have not cared enough to raise them up and ignite their lamp for them.

You and I have to answer this noble call. First we have to believe that we have something special that we can share with someone. It does not have to be money; it can be a piece of advice, a phone call, a pearl of wisdom, an idea, a connection, a listening ear, etc. It could be anything that will help them achieve their dream or at least set them on the right path.

Marianne Williamson, the author of 'A return of Love' said:

Our deepest fear is not that we are inadequate. Our deepest fear is that we are powerful beyond measure. It is our light, not our darkness, that most frightens us. We ask ourselves, who am I to be brilliant, gorgeous, talented, fabulous? Actually, who are you not to be? You are a child of God. Your playing small doesn't serve the world. There's nothing enlightened about shrinking so that other people won't feel insecure around you. We are all meant to shine, as children do. We were born to make manifest the glory of God that is within us. It's not just in some of us; it's in everyone. And as we let our own light shine, we unconsciously give other people permission to do the same. As we're liberated from our own fear, our presence automatically liberates others.

As farfetched as this may seem to some of you reading this book, still I urge you to give it the benefit of the doubt and begin to believe that you have got something great and truly amazing inside of you and begin to take steps to start sharing your resources, your light, your joy, your connections with other people, with the intention of helping them through their life journey.

Nothing has given me more joy and positive energy than helping some young people to pursue their dreams. I have counted it a privilege and an honour to hear people say the reason they succeeded was because I helped them. It melts my heart and honestly humbles me to the knees.

In life, one of the major laws of increase is 'the law of increase by association.' This law is universal and it's very effective. If you want to succeed, just hang out with successful people and do what they do. If you want to fail, just start knocking about with losers and inevitably you will become one of them. This is why it is not advisable to form an alliance with people who have opposite fundamental beliefs to you. As you know, light and darkness can not coexist and only an iron can sharpen another iron, wood can not sharpen an iron. Get people who have similar goals as you and encourage and challenge each other in a healthy way. If you're a successful person and you spend a lot of your time with nine losers you'll become the tenth in no time.

You have to be conscious of the fact that no relationship produces a neutral result. If a relationship does not increase you, it will inevitably decrease you.

A study by Massachusetts Institute of Technology indicated that a student who had no previous record of depression started showing signs of depression when he was paired as a roommate with another student who suffered from depression. This is called emotion contagion. Be careful who you link with and allow into your life. Find someone who wants to do what you have become a master at and teach them, and on the flipside, find somebody who has achieved what you want to accomplish and attach yourself to them to learn all that you need to know in order to succeed. This guarantees happiness for both parties.

SECURE YOUR FUTURE

I believe that every person is a leader in their own right. Although responsibilities and job titles may be different, we all still need to bring something to the table and lead ourself and each other in order to make our community or company a thriving place.

Every leader knows that they have no future unless they can raise somebody up to whom they will pass the baton of leadership. The reason some businesses fail is simply because the 'old leader' has not taken the time to plant a seed of leadership in somebody who could one day take over from them. An excellent leader is one who secures his/her future by investing in a protégé.

Who is learning from you? Who are you coaching or mentoring? What will happen to the great edifice that you're building now when you're gone? My guess is that everything you're putting in place now will all be disregarded and torn down as soon as you're gone and replaced by somebody else, unless you replicate yourself in somebody who will carry your goal and vision a step further.

I watched a reality show which featured lots of multi-millionaires and some billionaire bosses who went undercover in their own companies with the intention of finding out what really goes on in their companies and to also find the real unsung heroes of the company. What was interesting about all the bosses but one is that they have all taken over from their parents. From the interviews, it was clear that their fathers had instilled in them work ethics and values, discipline and tenacity, and furnished them with all the success secrets that they need to take their individual companies into the future. Who is going to take over from you? Whoever takes over from you is the person that will truly miss you when you're gone. It is that person or group of people that will be your living legacy.

This is the way to secure your future. Don't get lost in your own glory, doing everything by yourself and telling everybody how wonderful you are. We already know how fabulous you are but your light will shine even brighter if you give everyone around you a piece of your light. Imagine you are alone holding a lit candle in the night that is as dark as Erebus. How much difference would your one candle make? Now imagine if you hand out five hundred lit candles to people, and they all take their positions. How much difference do you think the five hundred lit candles would make? I believe the difference would be an incredible one.

Are you ready to transform your life and release 'the imprisoned splendour'? In five years time will you still be where you are today or will you have created the best version of yourself and emerged into your greatness? You can not afford to hold back now because somcone locked down by ignorance and crippled by fear is waiting for you to play the hero who saves them.

I would like to share the words of Maya Angelou et al with you:

I know that since life is our most precious gift and as far as we can be absolutely certain it's given to us to live but once, that as so live we will not regret years of useless virtue, inertia, and timidity and ignorance. And in our last moments we can say, all my life, all my conscious energies have been dedicated to the most noble cause in the world which is the liberation of the human mind and spirit, beginning with my own

I do sincerely hope that you won't wait till the end of your time here on earth before you can say that your life and conscious energies are completely dedicated to the liberation of the human mind and you're beginning with your own. I urge you today not to take the greatness inside you to the grave. The graveyard is already full of wealth of ideas and inventions that were never created. Myles Munroe said the richest place on the earth is the graveyard. Don't take your gifts and talents there. Use up all your wealth to make this world a better place and leave behind a path others can take.

This is your chance. You stand on the verge of an amazing transformation into an enlightened, empowered and a focused You. And when that happens, it can only mean one thing: You will be the best version of yourself and you will be unstoppable, and best of all you will become a BLESSING to others.

I want to leave you with these blessings: "…May the road rise to meet you… May love and laughter light your days and warm your heart and home. May good and faithful friends be yours wherever you may roam. May peace and plenty bless your world with joy that long endures. May all life's passing seasons bring the best to you and yours"

Time to Take Action

It is not enough to say this book is a good book and everything you read in it has been inspiring and challenging, although this is all well and good and it makes me feel very humbled and privileged to have come into your world to share these incredible truths with you. It will be priceless and it will mean more to me if you could take the eternal principles and truths in this book and use them to transform your life and become the best version of yourself. The world and the people around you are all tired of the fake you. I believe you are tired of the fake you too, especially when you know that if you try hard enough and persist, you could become a better you and achieve your dream.

A better you is achievable because the seed is already inside you. You do not have to be held back by the past or be dazed and confused by the future. All you have to do is find that core within you and fan it into flame. In the words of Oliver Holmes, "what lies before us and what lies ahead of us are tiny matters compared to what lies within us". There is a reason why your maker made you so. Time is ticking and "life is too short to be little". Dream Big and Take Action. You have now been enlightened and empowered to succeed and to be truly happy and be the BEST YOU. You have a PURPOSE in life and the POWER to fulfill your purpose has been put in you and we are all now awaiting your amazing and unlimited POSSIBILITIES.

<u>My Goals</u>

✓

✓

✓

✓

If you learn to ignore the wrong things and focus on the right ones this is what you'll see:

It is

_{im}POSSIBLE!

Website: www.josephafolabi.com

Twitter: @josephafolabi1

Made in the USA
Charleston, SC
08 November 2012